The ABC'S

With

Lolly's Angels

Viola J. Larimore

Photography by Sarah Bottarel

www.sarahbottarelphotography.com

Balboa Press books may be ordered through booksellers or by contacting:

Balboa Press
A Division of Hay House
1663 Liberty Drive
Bloomington, IN 47403
www.balboapress.com
1 (877) 407-4847

ISBN: 978-1-5043-4568-2 (sc)
ISBN: 978-1-5043-4569-9 (e)

Library of Congress Control Number: 2015919274

Print information available on the last page.

Balboa Press rev. date: 11/30/2015

BALBOA
PRESS
A DIVISION OF HAY HOUSE

In January 2014, it was placed upon my heart to write a poem for my grand-angels. As I would drift off to sleep at night I would reflect on words that could be used in the poem that would help them learn, combined with phrases that I say to inspire and guide them through life.

Once all the words were in place, I typed the poem and put it in a frame for them to hang on the wall. As I looked at the poem I began to see that it was not just a poem in a frame, it was to be bigger than that. Quickly, I imagined that the poem could become a photo book and given to them as a keepsake, but after awhile it became clear it was to be even more. These words could be published in a book with pictures and it could be shared with other kids of all ages!

It is my hope that your hearts be filled with love and inspiration as you share these words with your little Angel!

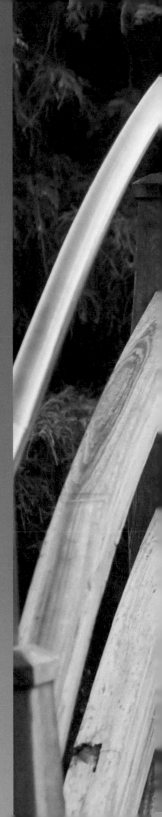

A is for ANGELS
sent from Above,

B is for BEAUTIFUL

hearts full of love.

C is the CRAZY

fun things that we do,

D is for DREAMS

we wish to come true.

E is your EYES

so big and so bright,

F is your FINGERS

that hold my hand tight.

G is the GARDEN

we grow things to eat,

H is for HEAVEN

where all Angels meet.

I is IMAGINE

your life at its best,

J is your JOY
when you see how
you're blessed.

K is show KINDNESS
in big ways and small,

L is show LOVE

for one and for all.

M is the MAGIC

we find in each day,

N is for NATURE

the best place to play.

O is to OPEN

your eyes and you'll see,

P is you're PERFECT

as PERFECT can be.

Q is to QUIETLY

gaze at a star,

R is for RAINBOW

a promise afar.

S is you're SMART
because you know why
you're here,

T is to TREASURE

those far and near.

U is the UNIVERSE

we share with each other,

V is so VERY

much to discover.

W is the WORLD

you make a better place,

X is the EXTRA

big smile on your face.

Y is for YOU
that I wrote this rhyme,

Z is life ZOOM'S

take one step at a time.

Reflections From My Heart

To my Mom, although not able to bear children herself, she answered the calling from God to be the Mommy to a little red-headed baby girl. She was so proud of her little Viola and provided so much love and tenderness that words cannot describe. I know that this book has her smiling from Above!

===

To my Dad, my very own Hometown Hero, I salute you for serving our Country as well as our community. What an honor for me to have you in my book!

===

To Miss Jaxsyn, my Heavenly Grand-Angel, although your life here on earth was so brief, you brought such joy and compassion to this world and you will always be a very special part of our family!! You truly make the world a better place!

About the Author

Viola J Larimore grew up in Fredonia, Kansas. Being a very curious little girl, she was always asking questions about one thing or another. Her Dad would often respond to her with, "Are you writing a book?" Who knew that one day his question to her would become a reality with this very book!

As a young adult, Viola moved to Springfield, Mo where she met her husband, Robert. In June of 2014, Viola and Robert celebrated 30 years as husband and wife on the beautiful island of Maui. It wasn't long after their magnificent adventure that Viola realized the little poem she wrote was to be shared with the world. She will always believe in the magic of Maui!

Viola and Robert live in Marshfield, Mo where they are blessed to be called Lolly and Pops by their amazing grand-angels! A very special "Thank You" to Pops for believing in Lolly's crazy notion to publish this book!

Printed in the United States
By Bookmasters